Four Virginia Poets Laureate

(2004-2012)

An Anthology & Reader's Guide

Sofia M. Starnes, Editor

Foreword by
Charles W. Steger, President of Virginia Tech

The Poetry Society of Virginia

Library of Congress Control Number 2012946934

978-0-9839192-6-1

Published by Cedar Creek Publishing
Linda M. Layne, Publisher
P. O. Box 115 • Bremo Bluff, Virginia 23022
www.cedarcreekauthors.com

Proofreader: Laurie Jensen - Anne's River Media

Printed in the USA

CONTENTS

Foreword

The power of the written word can transform the human experience. It does so in many ways. Whether they convey our sense of values as in the *Declaration of Independence* or the laws that express the tenets of civilized society, words shape our thoughts and behavior. Within this broad context of both the spoken and written word, poetry occupies a special place. How and what we write affects how we think. As holistic individuals, we must employ all dimensions of our intellect to navigate the complex array of concepts and experiences we encounter.

Deductive reasoning, inductive reasoning, associative reasoning, seeing, hearing, and feeling with all our senses come into play. Sometimes the range of experiences is overwhelming. The poems contained in this anthology embody a complex context which defines a broad range of feeling and perceptions of reality. One of the special roles of poetry is to concentrate observations and their attendant emotions in ways that can be a powerful stimulus to our imagination and help us to transcend the particular moment of occurrence.

The Poets Laureate of Virginia featured in this anthology possess this special gift. Our lives are richer for their dedication to their craft as well as the insights from their hearts.

Charles W. Steger
President
Virginia Tech

The Recovery of Poetry: One Poem at a Time

Joseph Brodsky once wrote that there are worse crimes than burning books; one of those crimes is not reading them. The reason behind this wisdom is that few sins of omission are more damaging to humanity than the failure to recognize beauty. And beauty is what great literature, especially poetry, makes available to the human heart.

The inability to become acquainted with the beauty in poetry means that we could easily miss the beauty in us, where it is left to slumber and expire unawakened. This is what we must avert at all cost. And we do so every time we read a poem to a friend, or introduce a poet to a young student, or forward a poetry link to our favorite web addict. After all, it is incumbent upon us, poets and poetry lovers alike, to keep that beauty, seen and expressed by poets, in society's field of vision at all times.

True beauty is never fleeting, which is why poetry demands thoughtful reading—as well as the gift of time. That is its challenge. Hence, when the Poetry Society of Virginia asked me to edit this anthology, I decided to keep those demands of time and of thought foremost in my mind. The poems would be a gift to the reader, for whatever time and setting he or she could provide. But each poem also would be accompanied by an invitation to ponder, to wander into the poet's creative space, for further understanding. To paraphrase Augustine of Hippo: in order to know, one must love, and the more one loves, the more one wishes to know. Reading a poem is an act of love, and the desire to enter more fully into the poem by understanding the creative process behind it is a natural consequence of that love.

It has certainly been an act of love—and a joy—to read and reread the extraordinary work of our most recent poets laureate for this anthology: Rita Dove, Carolyn Kreiter-Foronda, Claudia Emerson, and Kelly Cherry. Pondering the linguistic journey behind the poems, in order to formulate some appropriate and useful invitations to ponder, also has been a joyous, albeit challenging, task. The challenge arises because readers of poetry come in all shapes, ages, backgrounds, and interests. They, and we, inhabit classrooms and reading rooms, gather in coffee shops and around kitchen tables; attend poetry readings and organize book clubs; teach and learn, whether we have just turned fifteen or wish we could turn fifty again. This anthology is for all of us.

A wider readership imposes its own limitations in detail and in depth. However, the book has much from which a reader might choose. If it is used in a classroom setting, I hope the teacher will find in the *Consider this* section ample and varied resources. The same may be said for a workshop or seminar setting, where the leader may wish to select the points best suited to the group. And if a bevy of friends gathers around the poems, for the joy of verse, here, too, the reader should find something to stir the probing process. Over and over, the underlying questions that I have posed are these: What occurs within the poem that does not occur elsewhere? How is language transformed and how does it transform us?

In addition to the points to ponder that follow each of the poems, readers will find something else to enrich their understanding of the poems. The anthology contains excellent commentaries by four outstanding writers: Kevin Elrod Quashie introduces us to Rita Dove as a Renaissance writer; Cathryn Hankla rightfully positions Carolyn Kreiter-Foronda's work in the great tradition of lyric poetry; Betty Adcock's remarks bring us closer to the wide-ranging rootedness of Claudia Emerson's work; and Fred Chappell draws us into Kelly Cherry's love poems in a mode both fresh and profound. Each of these commentators chose their topic and their approach with no limitations from this editor. Their offerings expand the scope of the book and offer further avenues by which to explore the work of our poets laureate.

Although biographies of these poets abound on-line and in print, I have included brief sketches, which are meant to be no more than an introduction to their rich and extensive careers. Also included is a succinct history of the position of Poet Laureate in the Commonwealth, composed by Ed Lull, former president of the Poetry Society of Virginia and co-editor of the first anthology of Virginia Poets Laureate published in 2006. I am grateful to Ed for his highly informative and interesting contribution. My thanks also to Nancy Powell, another former president of the Poetry Society of Virginia. The project was conceived during her tenure, and she has lent invaluable support throughout the process; the book would not be what it is without her caring leadership.

I would like to extend very special thanks to Charles Steger, President of Virginia Tech, for his endorsement of this book, evident in his thoughtful foreword. President Steger sponsors the Steger Undergraduate Prize for Poetry at Virginia Tech, the largest such award for undergraduates in the nation, possibly in the world. His sponsorship of this honor is a statement of support for poetry that extends well beyond the Virginia Tech campus, to affect all of us, through its positive ripple effect.

Finally, and most importantly, we owe Rita Dove, Carolyn Kreiter-Foronda, Claudia Emerson, and Kelly Cherry an immense debt of gratitude. Their generous permission to reproduce their work in this anthology is but a sign of the liberality of their spirits, revealed further through their long and rich creative careers and their service as Poets Laureate of Virginia.

Sofia M. Starnes
Poet Laureate of Virginia, 2012-2014
Editor, *Four Virginia Poets Laureate 2004-2012: An Anthology & Reader's Guide*

Poet Laureate of Virginia: *A Brief History*

The Virginia legislature established the honorary position of Poet Laureate of Virginia on December 18, 1936, with appointments made by the General Assembly. The first poet honored was Carter Warner Wormeley (1874—1938), who was selected in December 1936 to serve as poet laureate for life. Each subsequent appointment was for a one-year term until the statute was changed in 1997.

The second poet so honored was Charles Day (1885—1946), who was appointed in 1942 for a one-year term. The position remained vacant for five years after that, until the General Assembly selected Thomas Lomax Hunter (1875—1948) to serve in 1948, and Leigh Buckner Hanes (1894—1967) for the year 1949. Following their tenures, Virginia had its first woman poet laureate, Ruby Altizer Roberts (1907—2004), who served her initial term in 1950. No further appointments were made for the next twenty years.

In February 1970, Guy Carleton Drewry (1901—1991) arrived at the post for a year-long term. After his service, the position lay once more dormant, although the General Assembly named Ruby Altizer Roberts Poet Laureate Emeritus in 1992. Kathryn Forrester Thro (b. 1954) was named to the position in July 1994, and served an extended term until June 1996. Margaret Ward Morland (b. 1923) was selected to serve in 1996. During her term, a new law was enacted in 1997, to the following effect:

7.1-43. Poet Laureate.

The honorary position of Poet Laureate of Virginia is hereby created. Beginning in 1998, the Governor may appoint a poet laureate from a list of nominees submitted by the Poetry Society of Virginia. Each poet laureate shall serve a term of two years with no restrictions on reappointment.

***Powers and Duties:** To encourage the exchange of arts information and perspectives. The poet laureate is not obligated to write any verse.*

Margaret Morland served as poet laureate until 1998. At the end of her tenure, Joseph F. Awad (1929—2009) was appointed for the following two-year term; Grace Simpson (b. 1931) served from 2000 to 2002, as did George Garrett (1929— 2008), who held the position from 2002 to 2004. These four poets are featured in the anthology published by the Poetry Society of Virginia in 2006, *Four Virginia Poets Laureate, a Teaching Guide.*

The first poet laureate of Virginia featured in this book is Rita Dove (b. 1952), a former poet laureate of the United States; she served as Virginia's poet laureate from 2004 to 2006. The Governor next appointed Carolyn Kreiter-Foronda (b. 1946) to fill the post from 2006 to 2008. Claudia Emerson (b. 1957) served the laureate appointment from 2008 to 2010. The final poet laureate featured in this book is Kelly Cherry (b. 1940), serving from 2010 to 2012. In 2012, Sofia M. Starnes was appointed Poet Laureate of Virginia, and currently holds that position.

Ed Lull
Former President
Poetry Society of Virginia

Rita Dove

2004-2006

RITA DOVE: A Biographical Sketch

Rita Dove was born in Akron, Ohio, in 1952. She received her BA from Miami University of Ohio before spending two semesters as a Fulbright scholar at Universität Tübingen in Germany. She subsequently joined the University of Iowa Writers' Workshop, where she earned her MFA degree in 1977.

Rita Dove's books include the poetry collections *The Yellow House on the Corner* (Carnegie-Mellon University Press, 1980), *Museum* (Carnegie-Mellon, 1983), *Thomas and Beulah* (Carnegie-Mellon, 1986), *Grace Notes* (W.W. Norton, 1989), *Mother Love* (W.W. Norton, 1995), *On the Bus with Rosa Parks* (W.W. Norton, 1999), *American Smooth* (W.W. Norton, 2004), and *Sonata Mulattica* (W.W. Norton, 2009). She also published *Fifth Sunday* (short stories, Callaloo Fiction Series, 1985), *Through the Ivory Gate* (a novel, Pantheon Books, 1992), and *The Poet's World* (essays, The Library of Congress, 1995). Her verse drama *The Darker Face of the Earth* (Story Line Press, 1994) received the Kennedy Center's New American Play Award and was first staged by the Oregon Shakespeare Festival in 1996, followed by productions at the Kennedy Center, the Royal National Theatre in London, and numerous other venues. *Seven for Luck*, a song cycle for soprano and orchestra with music by John Williams, premiered with the Boston Symphony Orchestra at Tanglewood in 1998. For the White House's "America's Millennium" celebration on New Year's Eve 1999, Rita Dove contributed a poem to Steven Spielberg's documentary *The Unfinished Journey*, which she read live from the Lincoln Memorial to a worldwide television audience. Her most recent publication is, as its sole editor, *The Penguin Anthology of 20th Century American Poetry* (2011).

Having previously been appointed US Poet Laureate and Consultant to the Library of Congress from 1993 to 1995 as well as Special Consultant for the Library of Congress's 200th anniversary in 1999/2000, Rita Dove served as Poet Laureate of the Commonwealth of Virginia from 2004 to 2006. Among her many literary and academic honors are the Pulitzer Prize in Poetry, the Emily Couric Leadership Award, the Heinz Award in the Arts and Humanities, the National Humanities Medal, the Common Wealth Award of Distinguished Service, Yale University's Chubb Fellowship, the Library of Virginia's Lifetime Achievement Award, the Fulbright Lifetime Achievement Medal, the Italian "Premio Capri" and 22 honorary doctorates.

Rita Dove is Commonwealth Professor of English at the University of Virginia in Charlottesville, where she lives with her husband, the writer Fred Viebahn. They have a grown daughter, Aviva Dove-Viebahn.

Persephone Abducted

She cried out for Mama, who did not
hear. She left with a wild eye thrown back,
she left with curses, rage
that withered her features to a hag's.
No one can tell a mother how to act:
there are no laws when laws are broken, no names
to call upon. Some say there's nourishment for pain,

and call it Philosophy.
That's for the birds, vulture and hawk,
the large ones who praise
the miracle of flight because
they use it so diligently.
She left us singing in the field, oblivious
to all but the ache of our own bent backs.

Consider this...

- "Persephone Abducted" is a sonnet, but what constitutes a sonnet? What are the two types of traditional sonnets and their particular rhyme schemes? Does this sonnet fulfill either of those schemes? If it doesn't, what makes it a sonnet? In answering, consider not only the sonnet's form but also its essence—one of which is that it should have a "twist" or "pivot?" Does this poem have such a twist? If so, where does it occur?

- Does the poet despise philosophy? Why or why not?

- Is the emotion at the beginning of the poem the same as the emotion at the end of the poem? Do you think a poem should express emotional movement? Why or why not?

- At times the subject of a verse in this poem is "she", other times the poet makes a general statement. Despite this dichotomy, how does the poet keep the poem focused?

Exit

Just when hope withers, a reprieve is granted.
The door opens onto a street like in the movies,
clean of people, of cats; except it is *your* street
you are leaving. Reprieve has been granted,
"provisionally"—a fretful word.

The windows you have closed behind
you are turning pink, doing what they do
every dawn. Here it's gray; the door
to the taxicab waits. This suitcase,
the saddest object in the world.

Well, the world's open. And now through
the windshield the sky begins to blush,
as you did when your mother told you
what it took to be a woman in this life.

Consider this...

- Whom is the poet addressing? How does the poet bring the reader into the poem? Through what poetic devices?

- Why is the suitcase the "saddest object in the world"? How does that statement contrast with the opening line of the final stanza? What does the contrast bring to light?

- Which verses of the poem are conversational, addressed to someone in particular, and which ones have the tone of universal statements? Is it important to strike a balance between the two? Why or why not?

- This poem has both images and metaphors. Select an image and a metaphor. What is the difference between the two?

Ach, Wien

The truly great cities are never self-conscious:
They have their own music; they go about business.
London surges, Rome bubbles, Paris promenades;
Dresden stands rigid, gazes skyward, afraid.

Vienna canters in a slowly tightening spiral.
Golden facades line the avenues, ring after ring
tracing a curve as tender and maddening
as a smile on the face of a beautiful rival.

You can't escape it; everywhere's a circle.
Feel your knees bend and straighten
as you focus each step. Hum along with it;
succumb to the sway, enter the trance.

Ah, sweet scandal: No one admits it.
but we all know this dance.

Consider this…

- Does this poem have a strict rhyme scheme? What about meter?
- Could you give examples of personification in the poem? What is the purpose behind this personification?
- What are some examples of emotional transference in the poem?
- Why do you think the poet chose the word "scandal" in the closing couplet?
- Think of a city or a town that you might describe through personification. Focus on its personality, its mode of expression, how this city or town makes you feel and act. Write a short poem about such a place. Are you using personification in your poem?

Against Flight

Everyone wants to go up—but no one can imagine
what it's like when the earth smoothes out, begins

to curve into its own implacable symbol.
Once you've adjusted to chilled footsoles,

what to do with your hands? Can so much wind
be comfortable? No sense

looking around when you can see
everywhere: There'll be no more clouds

worth reshaping into daydreams, no more
daybreaks to make you feel larger than life;

no eagle envy or fidgeting for a better view
from the eighteenth row in the theater...

no more theater, for that matter, and no
concerts, no opera or ballet. There'll be

no distractions except birds,
who never look you straight in the face,

and at the lower altitudes,
monarch butterflies—brilliant genetic engines

churning toward resurrection in a foreign land.
Who needs it? Each evening finds you

whipped to fringes, obliged to lie down
in a world of strangers, beyond perdition or pity—

bare to the stars, buoyant in the sweet sink of earth.

Consider this...

- How does the use of couplets affect the poem?
- Count the negatives. What impact does the profusion of "no" and "never" have?
- Which verse changes the tone—the emotional tenor—of the poem?
- Consider the phrase: "beyond perdition or pity..." How does the alliteration focus the verse? Read the next line and notice another alliteration: "bare...buoyant." What impact does the device have here? Identify other alliterations.
- Are there assonances as well in the poem? If so, point them out. Do you think that assonances and alliterations produce different emotional effects? Feel the sounds in your head before you answer.

"I have been a stranger in a strange land"

> *Life's spell is so exquisite, everything*
> *conspires to break it.*
> —Emily Dickinson

It wasn't bliss. What was bliss
but the ordinary life? She'd spend hours
in patter, moving through whole days
touching, sniffing, tasting…exquisite
housekeeping in a charmed world.
And yet there was always

more of the same, all that happiness,
the aimless Being There.
So she wandered for a while, bush to arbor,
lingered to look through a pond's restive mirror.
He was off cataloging the universe, probably,
pretending he could organize
what was clearly someone else's chaos.

That's when she found the tree,
the dark, crabbed branches
bearing up such speechless bounty,
she knew without being told
this was forbidden. It wasn't
a question of ownership—
who could lay claim to
such maddening perfection?

And there was no voice in her head,
no whispered intelligence lurking
in the leaves—just an ache that grew
until she knew she'd already lost everything
except desire, the red heft of it
warming her outstretched palm.

Consider this…

- Are you familiar with the creation story in the Book of Genesis? If not, find and read the text as a literary piece. What elements of that story surface in this poem?

- Both Genesis and the poem are sustained metaphors. What is behind the sustained metaphor of this poem?

- There are both ideas and emotions in this poem; could you identify each? How does the poet strike a balance between thought and sentiment?

- Does the emotion of the poem convey a reality that exceeds individual experience?

Golden Oldie

I made it home early, only to get
stalled in the driveway-swaying
at the wheel like a blind pianist caught in a tune
meant for more than two hands playing.
The words were easy, crooned
by a young girl dying to feel alive, to discover
a pain majestic enough
to live by. I turned the air conditioning off,
leaned back to float on a film of sweat,
and listened to her sentiment:
Baby, where did our love go?-a lament
I greedily took in
without a clue who my lover
might be, or where to start looking.

Consider this...

- What is the truth at the heart of this poem that goes beyond the specific experience? Could you tell, in the form of prose, what has just happened in the poem? What is the difference between your prose narrative of those events and the making of a poem?

- How do sounds make a poem? Can you identify any rhymes, both end rhymes and internal rhymes?

- Think of synonyms for the following words: majestic, crooned, float, sentiment, and greedily. Would those synonyms work as effectively in the poem as the words the poet used? Why or why not?

Lady Freedom Among Us

don't lower your eyes
or stare straight ahead to where
you think you ought to be going

don't mutter *oh no*
not another one
get a job   fly a kite
go bury a bone

with her oldfashioned sandals
with her leaden skirts
with her stained cheeks and whiskers and
                                        heaped up trinkets
she has risen among us in blunt reproach

she has fitted her hair under a hand-me-down cap
and spruced it up with feathers and stars
slung over her shoulder she bears
the rainbowed layers of charity and murmurs
all of you   even the least of you

don't cross to the other side of the square
don't think *another item to fit on a tourist's agenda*

consider her drenched gaze   her shining brow
she who has brought mercy back into the streets
and will not retire politely to the potter's field

having assumed the thick skin of this town
its gritted exhaust its sunscorch and blear
she rests in her weathered plumage
bigboned   resolute

don't think you can forget her
don't even try
she's not going to budge

no choice but to grant her space
crown her with sky
for she is one of the many
and she is each of us

Consider this…

- Why do you think there are no punctuation marks in the poem? What is the emotional effect of this device?
- In this poem, too, the poet uses the negative repeatedly. Does this usage have the same impact as it does in "Against Flight"?
- Is this a narrative poem or a lyrical poem? Explain your answer.
- Make a list of images that give "Lady Freedom Among Us" a physical identity and a personality. Why were they selected?
- How does the poet apply synecdoche in this poem? Give several examples.

The Event

Ever since they'd left the Tennessee ridge
with nothing to boast of
but good looks and a mandolin,

The two Negroes leaning
on the rail of a riverboat
were inseparable: Lem plucked

to Thomas' silver falsetto.
But the night was hot and they were drunk.
The spat where the wheel

churned mud and moonlight,
they called to the tarantulas
down among the bananas

to come out and dance.
You're so fine and mighty; let's see
what you can do, said Thomas, pointing

to a tree capped island.
Lem stripped, spoke easy: Them's chestnuts,
I believe. Dove

quick as a gasp. Thomas, dry
on deck, saw the green crown shake
as the island slipped

under, dissolved
in the thickening stream.
At his feet

a stinking circle of rags,
the half-shell mandolin.
Where the wheel turned the water

gently shirred.

Consider this...

- In her introduction to *Thomas and Beulah*, Rita Dove gives the following directive to the reader: "These poems tell two sides of a story and are meant to be read in sequence." We must therefore read this poem carefully, knowing that there is more elsewhere. Nevertheless, as you read this poem, which is the first in the book, are you able to understand and appreciate it as a poem by itself? Why or why not?

- Some poems draw us into a specific scene, others set the scene apart. What does "The Event" do? Does the poet create a sense of inclusion or of separateness? Point to specific verses for each response.

- Think of the various explicit and implicit colors in the poem. How many different colors do you see in your mind, as you read the poem? Knowing the poet's concern with issues of race, do you think the presence of these colors is meant to widen the scope of the poem or to focus it?

- Notice the presence of the mandolin in the opening and closing stanzas. What does this recurrence do for the poem? Is the image of the mandolin the same at the beginning and at the end of the poem? Is the mood each projects different? Support your answer.

- Much later, in *Thomas and Beulah*, we learn that Lem dies in "The Event." Is there any element within the poem that intuits this tragedy?

Poetry as Renaissance: The Work of Rita Dove

Rita Dove is a renaissance unto herself, a writer whose work represents boldness and excellence, as she portrays that which is beyond us and that which is acutely characteristic of our humanity. In nine collections of poetry spanning 30 years, she never merely offers up terrific single poems but always angles toward telling the whole story about what it means to be alive, so that her poems become narratives of a life lived: the struggle for a mother to love and let go; the study of the everyday people who shaped a civil rights movement; the tale of a nineteenth-century biracial musical genius, where we read of love, friendship, betrayal, and the way race and privilege contributed to the making of the modern world. And so the best word to describe Dove's work might well be "epic," as Homer's *The Odyssey* is epic. Or Herman Melville's *Moby Dick* and Toni Morrison's *Beloved* are epic. Or Dove's own giant book *Thomas and Beulah.*

Thomas and Beulah, Dove's masterful collection, which was awarded the Pulitzer Prize in Poetry in 1986, is a gathering of poems about her maternal grandparents. The book is magnificent for its narration of love, desire, and disappointment. Critics have remarked on the way Dove's expertise gives both Thomas and Beulah their own unique fullness. That is, she avoids the expected sentimental story of two black people whose love for each other bolsters them against the violence of the twentieth century. Instead, she looks into the inner life of two human beings who are joined in marriage but whose interiors remain their own. This idea of the interior is important to Dove's work, because in poem after poem

Dove is determined to have us peek into the innermost desires, ambitions, and vulnerabilities of her subjects.

Thomas and Beulah is meant to be read as a sequence: twenty-three poems about Thomas's life, twenty-one about Beulah's. However, even as the lives of these two characters (and the poems) overlap, the moments in each section focus on the particularity of their experiences, and we read of Thomas's and Beulah's specific relationships to everyday mundanity and to the awe of living.

"The Event" is the first poem in the Thomas section, and it sets up the reader's understanding of how a moment from boyhood will shape, quietly, the rest of the central character's life. In this poem, Dove uses subtle formal structures to help guide the rhythm and sentiment of the anecdote. Notice, for example, that the stanzas are all tercets, except for the last one which is a single line. This form allows the poem to move quickly, with excitement, while it uses lots of rhyme, especially in words that echo each other's sounds obliquely. (We say "obliquely" or "slant" when the rhymes are not exact.)

Notice also how Dove uses line breaks and punctuation to enhance the sense of closeness and the devastation of separation. For example, after the poem tells us that the two boys were "inseparable," a colon distinctly, yet slyly, introduces their separation—"Lem plucked / to Thomas' silver falsetto." This is an example of enjambment, when a phrase, clause or idea is broken up at the end of a line or stanza.

Enjambment is used in other places of the poem as well ("Thomas, dry / on deck, saw the green crown shape / as the island slipped / under") and each of these repeated separations points to the dramatic final line: single, alone, and widowed. The poem is beautiful and simple and haunting; everything that it describes happens in a quick and quiet way, which is also, through Dove's poetic craft, the way the poem unfolds.

These features of "The Event" are noticeable throughout Dove's work. Dove has a deep appreciation of how a particular poetic form or genre can shape content—as is the case with the various sonnets included in this anthology ("*Ach*, Wien," "Exit," "Persephone Abducted," and "Golden Oldie"). But her interest in form also relates to how rhyme, punctuation, and repetition can enhance meaning, often in ways that are unconscious to the reader, as in the relatedness and iteration of "back," "hawk," and "backs" in "Persephone Abducted." Or how the deliberate use of a specific stanza length can imply movement, as in the couplets of "Against Flight," a poem that also ends in a single widow line. In "Lady Freedom Among Us," Dove shows us that the absence of punctuation or capitalization has its valuable uses. Here, it creates a speaker whose voice feels immediate and intimate and wise; it also enhances the poem's persistent pace.

It is not only form but also the specificity of diction that matter in Dove's work. A great example is the use of the word "withered" in "Persephone Abducted." This word, "withered," works to amplify other terms in the poem: abduction, nourishment, even oblivious. The opening sound of "withered"—*with*—is notable, for it implies togetherness, which is somewhat contrary to the meaning of the word. It gives us an instance of intensification through contrast. The concept of "withering" is picked up again in the poem "Exit," although here it serves to strengthen another dynamic word—"reprieve." Repeatedly, in Dove's poetry, the particularity of language matters as much as form.

Dove's aesthetic is also notable for the way she considers race, that she does not imagine blackness as separate from what we think of as classical, does not distinguish the vernacular from the royal. The characters in her poems think and speak in various languages and idioms, some European and old, some African and older, some from jazz or bluegrass, some from words passed along on a small city street. In the book *Museum*, we find Benjamin Banneker next to William Shakespeare; in *Yellow House on the Corner*, Kentucky is as much a place as Tunisia. Dove uses the Greek myth of Persephone to express the intimacy of a mother's love; she takes on the reinterpretation of Eve's stunning choice in the Biblical garden; she works in a reference to a line from the Supremes (in "Golden Oldie"), traces the great cities of Europe (in "*Ach,* Wien"), and connects the Venus of Willendorf to her meditation on black civil rights. Finally, in "Against Flight," she lays out a map of the endless atmosphere of the cosmos. Dove's poems encompass not only the world, but also the heavens.

Rita Dove does all of this without sacrificing accessibility in her work. She is clear and readable, because she is interested in saying something about the experience of being human. There is an element of dailyness in this poet's poems, as if they were pieces of music, at once conceptual and hummable; they are able to inspire because they find their way intimately into a reader's mind. These are not stuffy poems intended for complex analysis about what is happening or what is being said. (A good example is "Golden Oldie," which tells us of the common experience of listening to an old beloved song on the car radio.) Nevertheless, the poems are chocked full of poetic expertise.

Dove is a renaissance unto herself because, while she writes poetry about sweeping arcs of time, she also represents life in its everyday smallness, including what it means to suffer indignity, and what it is to have agency.

Life is vulnerability and capacity, a point exemplified in "Heart to Heart" from *American Smooth.* This poem begins with the observation that the heart is not at all as we often represent it—red or sweet or capable of breaking or melting. It, the heart, is "just a thick clutch / of muscle, / lopsided, / mute." The poem continues:

> Still,
> I feel it inside
> its cage sounding
> a dull tattoo:
> *I want, I want*—
> but I can't open it:
> there's no key.
> I can't wear it
> on my sleeve,
> or tell you from
> the bottom of it
> how I feel. Here,
> it's all yours, now—
> but you'll have
> to take me,
> too.

Again, Dove shows herself to be in control of her craft, in the use of poetic features: line breaks, pace, movement. But beyond these, what is exceptional in "Heart to Heart" is how accurately the poem describes what is nearly indescribable: the risk and thrill of desire. Dove characterizes the heart's beating as a two-word phrase, "I want, I want," a brilliant metaphor for the yearning that lives in us. The phrase "I want" is an iambic phrase, two beats, one with a stressed emphasis, which is what makes iambic so natural a register in the English language—it mimics the heartbeat. Dove, so astute a writer, gets this; Dove, so capable and generous a human, writes this lesson down for our taking. She has the intellect to imagine great narratives and ideas, and the skill to detail them in exquisite, accessible language.

If you look up the word renaissance, not as an adjective but as a noun, you will read the following definitions: the spirit and activity of a great revival, the marking of modernity, a resurgence, any renewed interest in learning and culture, in the fruits of humanity. Truly, this is what best characterizes Rita Dove's poetry, a renaissance unto itself.

Kevin Everod Quashie

Carolyn Kreiter-Foronda

2006-2008

CAROLYN KREITER-FORONDA: A Biographical Sketch

A native of Farmville, Virginia, Carolyn Kreiter-Foronda graduated from Mary Washington College (now the University of Mary Washington) with a BA in English, and received two master's degrees and a PhD from George Mason University, the first doctorate presented by the school. She received a Virginia Educational Research Award for her dissertation.

Carolyn Kreiter-Foronda's work has appeared widely, both in journals and anthologies, among them *Nimrod International Journal, The Ledge, Anthology of Magazine Verse & Yearbook of American Poetry, WPFW 89.3 FM Poetry Anthology, Blood to Remember: American Poets on the Holocaust, Best of the Literary Journals, An Endless Skyway: Poetry from the State Poets Laureate, Dominion Review, Hispanic Culture Review, Prairie Schooner, Poet Lore, Mid-American Review, Antioch Review, Passages North, The Journal of Teaching Writing* and *The Writing Center Journal.* Her poetry collections are *Contrary Visions* (under the name, Carolyn Kreiter-Kurylo, Scripta Humanistica, 1988), *Gathering Light* (SCOP, 1993), *Death Comes Riding* (SCOP, 1999), *Greatest Hits* (Pudding House, 2000), and *River Country* (San Francisco Bay Press, 2008). She co-edited the anthology *In a Certain Place* and *Four Virginia Poets Laureate: A Teaching Guide*, a precursor of this book. Her forthcoming book features monologues in the voices of Mexican artists, Diego Rivera and Frida Kahlo. Dr. Kreiter-Foronda also has read her work at numerous universities, libraries, and cultural institutions in this country and abroad, including the Library of Congress (Hispanic Division), the Folger Shakespeare Library, and the American Embassy in Sofia, Bulgaria.

Carolyn Kreiter-Foronda's extensive service to the Commonwealth, in the areas of the arts and education, has garnered her numerous recognitions. She has received three Artist-in-Education grants from the Virginia Commission for the Arts, an Arts-on-the Road grant from the Virginia Commission for the Arts, an Edgar Allan Poe First Place poetry award, a Council for Basic Education fellowship award, the Fairfax County Public Schools' Hodgson Award in English, a National Scholastic Teacher Portfolio Award, and a Resolution of Appreciation awarded by Virginia's Board of Education, among other citations. In 2007, she was named Alumna of the Year at both of her alma maters, George Mason University and the University of Mary Washington. She served as Virginia's Poet Laureate from 2006 to 2008.

Dr. Kreiter-Foronda is currently working with Claudia Emerson on the Dulles Corridor Metrorail Public Art Project to highlight the poetry of eight Virginia Poets Laureate, as well as award-winning established and emerging state poets, in permanent art installations in three Northern Virginia metro stations. A practicing visual artist, she conducts ekphrastic poetry workshops throughout the country and teaches in the Statewide Partners Program for the Virginia Museum of Fine Arts.

Carolyn Kreiter-Foronda lives in Hardyville, Virginia, with her husband, Patricio.

Apples

Today I'm thinking of apples,
a country kitchen, the smell

of pie cooling in the late
summer air. Let's say

it's evening, the hour
when anything's possible.

A small girl in a hammock
dreams of lightning: *poor will,*

poor will, a horse's whinny
in the air. She wakes

to a wind, apples thrown
to the earth: succulent globes

that she rubs and rubs
until the world shines.

I'd like to say this happened
the first time a woman plucked

an apple and saw it as good.
I'd like to say she took the juices

of berries and painted a still
life that comes alive tonight

in the palms of a child,
the ripest fruit tilted

toward the light, ageless
and holding on.

Consider this...

- What kind of mood does this poem induce? How does the poet create such a mood?

- As you read the poem, do you find yourself inside the setting of the poem? If so, how did the poet draw you in? If not, in what way did the poet create a sense of separateness? Which verses support your response?

- The line breaks in this poem have produced short couplets. Does this hasten or delay your reading of the poem? What other effect might the format have?

- Like Rita Dove, in the previous section, Kreiter-Foronda references the Genesis story in this poem. Differentiate the aim and style of the poems.

- Poetry often juxtaposes the timeless with the temporal. Does this dichotomy occur in this particular poem? If so, in what way, through which verses?

A Basket of Potatoes

In the Andean heartland where potatoes
were first cultivated, they remain sacred
for the indigenous people.

All evening I've been in the root cellar
laying out potatoes on a bed of leaves.

How ritualistic this seems, bringing in
the crop from earth where it cured

for three nights in the cold mountain air.
I want to dance barefoot on this altar,

squish liquid from the fleshy tubers,
squeeze the soft skins between my toes

like an Indian preparing *chuño.* In the late
hour, it takes so little to weave a spell.

The potatoes gather the room's dimness,
their eyes vigilant as the new moon slips

through the door's slats. I lean down
and steady a potato in a thimbleful

of radiance. The scrolls of its life
palpable, the eyes heavy-lidded, it opens

like a flower in my mind. I see again
a Quechuan woman shrouded and ringed

in a halo of the bountiful crop.
I remember offering my relative a prayer.

If only I could have given her a basket
of tranquillity: *papas de regalo,*

gift potatoes, yellow to deep purple.
Always, I dream like this until

the dead cross over to a place where
even a disbeliever begins to dance.

Consider this…

- The poet uses "I" several times in the poem. How does this personal presence affect your reading?

- The poem does not seem to be only about the poet. What verses open it up to areas beyond the poet's experience? (If you disagree with the preceding statement and believe that the poem is exclusively about the poet, indicate why.)

- In creating the scene for the poem, the poet uses more than one sense. Give examples of how the imagery is derived from a wide range of sensual perceptions. Which do you find most effective? Why?

- In several couplets, the sounds of one word play off effectively against another. For example: "laying" and "leaves," or "squish" and "fleshy." Find other examples and evaluate their effect in the poem.

- The poet intersperses Spanish words in the poem. Why do you think she does this?

- Are you sufficiently familiar with a word in a different language that you might incorporate into a poem? If so, try it out. Build a poem in English around this word.

By the Bay

How easy to become
a part of this fertile past:
a vast, amazed sky, gulls
billowing their small white
sails, caught in impetuous
breezes. To be here
beyond a peninsula's tip
and a temple of wind,
where an inlet's waters
wash over my feet,
the Chesapeake misting over
with the aura of coastlands.
I call out from this Point
as if expecting honey,
vanilla, and tobacco
from a passing ship
to blow ashore in boxes.
What is it about the Bay
that startles the heart?
The clouds' wealth opens
up, each drop cleansing:
all at once I am washed
in translucent wine.

Consider this...

- The poet has elected to write this poem without any stanza breaks. Why do you think she did so? If you were to create breaks, where would you place them? How would that affect the poem?

- Several words in the poem give it an almost religious feel. Can you identify those words? Why do you think the poet used them? What is the difference between the religious and the sacred in poetry?

- The poet/persona takes several actions in the poem. Identify the verbs that describe those actions. Nature also is moved to action in the poem (the bay, the clouds, the water...). Make another list of those action verbs. Compare the action of nature with the action of the poet in the poem. What is the prevalent tone of each listing? In what way do the actions of the poet and those of nature intersect?

You Don't Need Binoculars to Be a Bird Watcher

Take Lake Nakuru in Kenya, the vast number
of flamingos. What greater bird than the Lesser:
carmine-red, the legs startle the water.

Perched on stilts, it slips
its bill beneath the surface, flips
its tongue into place, then dips

for algae. Outnumbered, the Greater towers
to six feet, feeds on mollusks, then clears
the lake, soars over tiers

of yellow acacias glinting in pure
sun. Rock-strewn hills, every detour
opens up on pelicans, seems an overture

to the view at the top: pink slides from sky
like a rainbow into your eyes
mesmerized by the flight. You ask why

there are so many birds rushing
to earth. Don't waste time looking
through binoculars. Start running

to the lake's edge for a closer view.
Look into the liquid heart where the blue-
green pulsates, red beaks sucking, then spew-

ing out water. Follow the pelicans' snow-white
ascent into the flamingos' flight.
Be like the birds. Lift. Ignite.

Consider this…

- Identify the structure of the poem and its rhyme scheme. What lines contain perfect rhymes? Which ones contain masculine rhymes and which have feminine rhymes?

- How does the use of rhymed tercets in a poem differ from the use of free verse? What effect does the pattern have on you, as a reader?

- Does this poem use end-stopped lines or run-on lines? Identify each of these and explain why you think the poet chose to use one over the other.

- How does the imagery of the poem outweigh the structure, so that the sensual perceptions prevail and remain with the reader?

Calla Lilies

After Desnudo con Alcatraces
(Nude with Calla Lilies), Diego Rivera

Kneeling on a petate mat,
The basket, deep enough,
an Indian woman sits upright,
supports our long, firm stems.
her unclothed frame scented.
We settle into clots of dirt.
Is it sandalwood? Mahogany?
Like absinthe, we intoxicate
I paint her broad shoulders:
the artist who shapes the woman's arms
earthy dabs of nutmeg, hyacinth
with the mastery of sun
so she can thrive like the flowers,
so she can embrace us.
so she can feel the florets swell.
Her hands smelling of freesia,
Soon, she will rise out of shadows
reach out to our trumpets blaring
to gather bluets, yarrows.
as though she hears a mariachi horn,
What is happiness, if not this need?
feels our desire to return to marshes,
See how she rests—a saint—holding
watery fields, shallow pools far from
pearls tamed like fire?
the lover who approaches a street vendor—
Now, maybe you understand who I am.
scissor snips ringing through the market,
In the city, in the valleys,
fleshy tubes and arrow-shaped leaves
I wander in search of legends
rolled into wrapping paper, sold for a few pesos,
to begin anew. Oh, these calla lilies!
the blooms' swanlike hearts pounding.

Consider this…

- This is a dual-voice poem. Join voices with another reader and read the poem aloud, alternating verses. Does each voice stand on its own as an independent poem? Why or why not?

- Identify the characteristics of each voice. Are they indicative? Imperative? Celebratory? Accusatory? What different emotions do they express?

- In a few sections of the poem, the voices appear to cross over each other creating a poetic braid. Could you identify where this occurs? How does the poet achieve this connection?

- What do you think was the aim of the poet in using the dual-voice form?

- Consider two characters in literature, history, or modern culture with whom you might identify. Write a short dual-voice poem to reflect those characters and their relationship with each other.

The Two Fridas, 1939

My blood is the miracle that travels in the veins
of the air from my heart to yours.
Frida Kahlo

As a child I met my imaginary friend
I have always known there are two of me:
in the earth's core O how she made me laugh
Dark-skinned Mexican My German self,
Before each secret romp, I blew on a window
strong-willed, blouse ripped open, heart undone,
in my room, the pane misty like blurry soap bubbles
scarlet flowers smeared on my skirt,
With my fingertip I drew a door, jumped through
its alabaster landscape stained I clamp a vein
to Pinzón Entering the store's giant O, I crawled
My indigenous sister clasps my hand,
into world's interior where a playmate opened her arms,
her other hand encircling a portrait: frog prince,
listened to my secret problems, consoled me,
Diego as a boy He lusts for the Mexican
made me laugh despite my burdens
His soul's yoked to hers That's
When it was time to leave, I erased the magical door
what tears us apart: veins, tethered, choke me,
from the glassy surface I wandered to the patio
our lives: aborted and miscarried
to sit beneath a cedar tree's dancing shadows
Stop this flow of shared blood Loosen this grip
to conjure her up again, sturdy as breath

Consider this...

- Although a poem stands on its own, we can enrich our knowledge of it by understanding its inspiration. Who was Frida? Do some research about this woman and her husband, the Mexican painter, Diego Rivera. Does your research explain why the author chose to give Frida two voices in the poem?

- Read the poem aloud with someone else, alternating voices. Now, paraphrase each section. Write out what the poem is telling you in prose. What did you have to disregard, in terms of style and poetic devices, in order to do so? What was lost in the change?

- The poem does not use end-rhymes, but there are several occasions of sounds playing off each other. Can you find them? What does this internal, at times subtle, pattern achieve in this poem, or in any poem?

Contrary Visions in the Gallery, *White on White*

. . . just a white surface that is simply
a white surface and nothing else.
Piero Manzoni

The child in the paisley frock remembers
the terrible storm, how her father saved
her, how suddenly the white winds came.
Stepping forward, she folds her hands
intently into a gesture of peace
like the dove, before her, darkening
the surface halfway across the canvas.

Beside her, two mystics vow
this is not the coming of light
or white blossoms at the hands of God,
but a ceremonial stone that brings calm
to any man, if only he will embrace it.

Whereas the artist intended nothing
of this, no more than a white surface,
the lilies I remember turn back years,
and I am a small child again,
comprehending the emptiness of white
offerings, their incantations cold
beside the burial ground. I am moved
by this stillness, by the beguiling white
canvas holding just enough light
to enfold this darkness, this grief.

Consider this...

- This is an ekphrastic poem, in other words, a poem inspired by a non-literary work of art, usually a visual work. If the title of the poem did not reveal its origin, at what point would you recognize this as an ekphrastic poem?

- How does the poet set the scene—through narration, description, or a combination of both?

- At what point does the poet establish a personal connection with the scene of the poem? How does she achieve this?

- Poetry has been described as an onion that one peels in search of another layer, only to find still another layer. Identify the layers in this poem. What is the core experience at the poem's closing?

- Having identified this core emotion, can you select at least five words in the poem that led you to it, or, in other words, that set the stage for the poem's parting sensation?

Hurricane

Where was fairness the night
your buckling gales snapped
the still-green trees?

Where was fairness
when woodland squirrels
wailed like brash screech

owls and deer lay paralyzed
in the heartless dark?
Was it fair to dream

of iridescent fields while
deafening whirlwinds
pillaged the land?

Fair to suffer a hurricane
twice: first as a frightened
child and again in autumn's rill?

Fair to rebuke you, tumbling
on your unwieldy path,
pushing turgid waters inland?

Fair to mull over your anger:
the jungle of pines, remnants
of homes washed to sea?

Fair to name you *consagrada*
a Dios? I remember squirrels
scampering in a flurry, their hurl

through branches of surviving oaks,
the unexpected, dawn-struck glory
bowed to this thriving earth.

Consider this…

- The word "fair" or "fairness" is used repeatedly in this poem. What is the impact of this repetition?
- Browse through a poetry anthology and find a poem by another poet, from any time in history, where the poet also uses repetition as a poetic device. Compare that poem to this one. See whether the device has more than one impact or purpose.
- Were you surprised by the poem's closing? How would you describe the shift in the emotion of the poem? How does the poet retain the poem's unity despite this closing shift?
- Listen to the sounds of the poem as if you were listening to a hurricane. Pick out the words that produce a galelike effect.

Solitude

River darkness descends like a rite
A resolute *kraa-kraa* unravels

the cloud-laden moon, picking
through thready reeds and cattails,

lambent in dusk. The marshes
murmur and swirl, startled

by the foot-stirring of a great egret.
Into rimmed air he glares,

alert for insects, crooks his neck
into a zigzag, and waits.

Loosening his breeding plumes,
he feathers shrub grasses,

his strong spear ready to plunge.
Bantam rays settle over plumage

of the bird stilled by a frog's croak,
by earth's heat dispersing night-croons.

In the shadows of laurel bushes,
I curl up like prey.

Skilled hunter, your golden
bill calls my name.

Consider this…

- A metonymy is a figure of speech where an aspect of an experience represents the whole experience—or a part represents the whole (also called synecdoche). Are there any instances of metonymy in this poem? If so, explain why/how they work.

- The word sounds in this poem also play an important role in conveying an experience. Can you give instances of onomatopeia?

- If the focus of the poem is on nature, why do you think it is titled "Solitude"? Is nature a passive or an active reality? Is there more stillness or more action? How are these conveyed?

- At the poem's conclusion, the poet becomes a part of nature. What role does she play?

Redoubled Visions: Carolyn Kreiter-Foronda's Lyrics

Carolyn Kreiter-Foronda's poems strike the ear along with the intelligence, evoking the natural world, visual art, and questions of self, transcendence, and responsibility, in the lyric mode. Her poems embrace the great subjects of the lyric: the intense, intuitive, and revelatory relationships that one thinking person can effect through observation, memory, and experience.

Lyrics are rooted in classical times when this type of poem was defined by accompanying strums on the lyre. The classical lyric separated itself from story-telling modes like elegies, epics and plays, and depended on personal and emotional experience rather than reason as its ground. We most often associate the lyric with its more modern incarnation in the English Romantic poets like Blake, Wordsworth, Coleridge, Shelley, and Keats, who took common folk and scenes as subjects along with their evolving examinations of self, memory, and the world around them. Wordsworth's definition, set forth in the Preface (1800) to the *Lyrical Ballads,* of poetry as "the spontaneous overflow of powerful feelings" penned by one who has "also thought long and deeply" remains a very present guide. Even as we quibble with the "spontaneous" part of the equation, we can see that Wordsworth was already backing off emotion alone when he added that one must also think deeply.

From the Romantic poets, contemporary readers and writers adopt the idea that poems often concern themselves with nature and the preservation of the natural, rendered in musical but common diction. Kreiter-Foronda is certainly a "nature poet," but more than this she is a poet who recognizes the web of connection between the human and natural worlds and the cost to the earth of hosting us. Gazing at nature and becoming awestruck doesn't end with the awe but delivers the poet to a deeper debt. The right action she demands is most often self-directed and moral, furnishing a thought correction. When the speaker rails at the storm's higher power in "Hurricane," she ends by turning the demand back on herself:

> Where was fairness
> when woodland squirrels
> wailed like brash screech
>
> owls and deer lay paralyzed
> in the heartless dark?
> Was it fair to dream
>
> of iridescent fields while
> deafening whirlwinds
> pillaged the land?
>
> Fair to suffer a hurricane
> Twice: first as a frightened
> child and again in autumn's rill?
>
> Fair to rebuke you, tumbling
> on your unwieldy path,
> pushing turgid waters inland?

The speaker recognizes mid-anger that the storm is only being itself, the best storm it can be. Rhetorical questions and sonic effects elevate the speech of the poem, especially assonance shifts from the *ea/a* to short *i/e* to the guttural *u*, but there is no multisyllabic or impressive vocabulary here, only well-selected nouns, verbs, and adjectives like "rill," "wailed," and "brash."

Lyrics have expanded poetry's audience and given poetry a personal and conversational tone, but this does not mean that they are always today written in free verse. Many traditional or received forms of poetry that are highly structured with meter and rhyme, such as sonnets and villanelles, are lyrics. So, we will find that contemporary lyric poets like to play around with form, either received or invented. Couplets can serve up a visual illustration of duality, one of Kreiter-Foronda's favorite themes, whether she explores human and nature, as she does in "Solitude," or imagination/dream and reality. Employing a form in which alternating lines imply couplets, as in the ekphrastic "Calla Lilies" and "The Two Fridas," she can create distinct attitudes or voices whose impact increases when the two strands weave as one. Both of these poems contain dual visions; italicized lines following the main strand present alternative readings as well as cultural alternatives in images of dark-skinned Mexican children or indigenous women as sister selves. This poet is also doubly gifted, doubly trained, and brings a painter's eye to the task of words. These partner-poems represent married partner-painters, Diego Rivera and Frida Kahlo, so one could interpret the double narratives as inspired by this marriage. Additionally, each poem contains an image of the other artist or surrogate for the other artist within it.

Kreiter-Foronda's poems like to use conversational form or address another person or force, as in "Hurricane" discussed above. The first half of "You Don't Need Binoculars to Be a Bird Watcher" takes pains to describe Lake Nakuru in Kenya where flamingos, greater and lesser, feed. In the second half, in a series of imperatives, the speaker impatiently implores a birder to come out from behind the scrim of binoculars and venture into nature itself: "Don't waste time looking / through binoculars. Start running // to the lake's edge for a closer view. / Look into the liquid heart where the blue-green / pulsates.... The poem ends ecstatically, "Be like the birds. Lift. Ignite." Indeed, the speaker's so insistent in this poem one might not notice the tercets or the way rhyme knits each set of lines in a triple pattern or the way the rhymes fall neatly on the line ends. End rhymes are good things to mask, and Kreiter-Foronda's good at understating her prosody to achieve a conversational tone. Sentence meanings continue despite the cutting of lines across sentences, while the sentences continue despite the stanza breaks:

> of yellow acacias glinting in pure
> sun. Rock-strewn hills, every detour
> opens up on pelicans, seems an overture
>
> to the view at the top: pink slides from sky
> like a rainbow into your eyes
> mesmerized by the flight. You ask why

Just look at all of that rhyme! But, when we listen to the poem read aloud the formal elements are not readily discerned. When lines cut against sentences and grammatical units, we say that the lines "run-on" or are enjambed. Sometimes a line, as an individual unit of sound and sense, offers up a new thought in itself, for example: "like a rainbow into your eyes" or "mesmerized by the flight. You ask why." One skillful way to manage rhyme is to employ run-ons like these, of lines and stanzas, to undermine the thudding effect of end-rhyme that can otherwise occur.

Retrospective and revelatory instincts in contemporary poetry draw upon Romantics like Rousseau and Wordsworth: the belief that the world can be made sense of in repose, as Wordsworth put it "emotion recollected in tranquility," or through the distance of memory. Images from the past and the phrase "I remember…" often enter Kreiter-Foronda's poems. In "By the Bay," the speaker imagines the sweep of the water and sky linking with what it ever was, and the Point becomes a point from which to contemplate the vastness of all creation:

> How easy to become
> a part of this fertile past:
> a vast, amazed sky, gulls
> billowing their small white
> sails, caught in impetuous
> breezes. To be here…

Similarly, in "A Basket of Potatoes" a shaft of light illuminates a tuber in the speaker's hands, which "opens // like a flower in my mind. I see again / a Quechuan woman shrouded and ringed // in a halo of the bountiful crop. / I remember offering my relative a prayer." The couplets of this poem illustrate past and present, but they also illustrate the essential connection of high and low. The tuber that comes out of the ground, the lowly potato, can conjure a spell or an exuberant dance. In this poem and in "Contrary Vision in the Gallery, *White on White*" intruding memories offer individual perspective, a contrasting or complementing experience from the past that subtly underscores the present situation as fleeting.

Prayer and grief are larger than the observed moment and can move through time and space. These poems seem to nudge us into being larger than we think we are, reminding us that our reach extends back to indigenous time through daily rituals, through something as ordinary as a potato stored in a root cellar. Or, by gazing at a seemingly blank painting, which presents nothing more to us than *white on white*, we can be transported to an experience of grief that was once all encompassing. Carolyn Kreiter-Foronda's poems locate themselves in the senses, in the sensory world, away from abstraction even when abstract art and a large emotion like grief is under contemplation. If one sense were more important than the others in her poems it would be seeing and visual imagery, and yet the poems rely heavily on the ear's tuning.

Kreiter-Foronda's poems remind us that seeing has its own way of meaning, and knowledge can arise from immersed observation as clearly as from overt acts of thinking. Her poems develop an idea of individual responsibility in relation to what is natural. In moments of intense emotion time is stilled, yet expands; these poems open like flowers with illuminated moments of double vision, inviting and challenging us to look again, revise our cursory sight and think more deeply.

Cathryn Hankla

Claudia Emerson

2008-2010

CLAUDIA EMERSON:
A Biographical Sketch

A native Virginian, Claudia Emerson was born in Chatham, a rural town southeast of the Blue Ridge mountains. She received her BA from the University of Virginia and an MFA from the University of North Carolina at Greensboro, where she was poetry editor for the *Greensboro Review*. She taught at Washington and Lee University and Randolph-Macon Women's College, before joining the faculty of Mary Washington College (now the University of Mary Washington) in Fredericksburg in 1998. She is the Arrington Distinguished Chair of Poetry and Professor of English and a contributing editor of the literary magazine *Shenandoah*.

Claudia Emerson's poems have been published widely, in such magazines as *Poetry*, *The Southern Review*, *The Georgia Review*, *TriQuarterly*, *Crazyhorse*, *New England Review*, and numerous other journals. In addition, her work has appeared in various anthologies, among them *Yellow Shoe Poets*, (LSU Press, 1999), *The Made Thing* (The University of Arkansas Press, 1999), *Buck and Wing: Southern Poetry at 2000*, (Shenandoah, 2000), *Strongly Spent: 50 Years of Shenandoah Poetry* (Shenandoah, 2003), and *Common Wealth: Contemporary Poets of Virginia* (University of Virginia Press, 2003). Her books of poems, *Pharaoh, Pharaoh* (1997) and *Pinion, An Elegy* (2002) were published as part of Louisiana State University Press's signature series, Southern Messenger Poets, edited by Dave Smith. Her most recent books, *Figure Studies* (2008) and *Secure the Shadow* (2012), also have been issued by LSU Press. In addition, Emerson is the editor of the anthology *Best New Poets* (University of Virginia Press, 2010).

In 2006, Claudia Emerson won the Pulitzer Prize for Poetry for her third collection *Late Wife*. She is one of only nineteen women to receive this honor—and the first southern woman ever to be so recognized. Previous recognitions include an Associated Writing Program's Intro Award, as well as an Academy of American Poets Prize, both awarded in 1991. Ms. Emerson has been granted individual artist's fellowships by the National Endowment for the Arts, the Library of Congress, and the Virginia Commission for the Arts. She received the Donald Justice Award from the Fellowship of Southern Writers in 2009 and in 2011 was inducted into the organization. She served as Poet Laureate of Virginia from 2008 to 2010.

Claudia Emerson lives in Fredericksburg, Virginia, with her husband, Kent Ippolito, a musician who plays with various types of bands, including bluegrass, rock, folk, jazz, blues, and ragtime.

Auction

Some things bring nothing. Later there will be
a bonfire of palm-worn plow handles.
But a doll, pallid—china hands fractured—
brings fifteen dollars.
                                        His bed they have hauled
out, the covers still on it, an old man's
nest of tangled flannel. I think he has
no daughters to know what must not be
sold. His late wife's dressing table gives up
its confused vanities: snaggletooth combs,
the warbled wire of hairpins, a lipstick,
a faint layer of blush over all. The sun-
shocked mirror denies this face, waves my hair,
widens my eyes, until I cannot see
the resemblance. Is this how she saw
herself? And over her shoulder the fields,
falling away from the house, steep with
distortion? Under her crushed narcissus,
the varicose wake of a mole heaves
as if the vagrant dead—grown bolder—rise,
thick palms bared for this shallow, movable darkness.

Consider this...

- The poet Tom Disch once wrote a poem titled "The Garage Sale as a Spiritual Exercise." Do you think this poem also could be titled "An Auction as a Spiritual Exercise"? If so, support your answer. If not, what do you think gives a particular poem a "spiritual dimension"?

- What kind of mood does the opening assertion "Some things bring nothing" create? Does the poem confirm this assertion?

- Select five images chosen by the poet to reflect a person's past life. Why do you think she selected those images?

- What was the reason for bringing the image of the fields "falling away from the house" into the poem?

- What is the role of "the mole" in the poem? Would the image of another animal do as well? Which one would you include? Why? How would the actions or characteristics of that particular animal alter the poem?

The Taxidermist

In good weather I herd them onto my lawn,
coats glossy, feathers bold. Cars slow for the fox
beside the quail, the bobcat by the sleeping
fawn. I turned each body inside out,
emptied it of flesh, fat, bones, eyes; the meat
of the lie displays the thin, defining skin
of something else. All that you see, I save.
Good enough to shoot again, you laugh,
but I know death is not held at bay, has not
even looked over its shoulder at the fleshing knives
and pliers, the saws and scalpels. This is tedious,
messy resurrection, and what I preserve
is not death or life or skill but the wounded
ghost of an old hunger that won't be tamed
and taught to lick your hand, old hunter, but will
bound through some finer field, beyond the wind
you foul, even as I rummage for the right
glass eye in drawered compartments. Here, see,
they are all here: loon, lynx, buck, fox, quail,
snake, and coon. All measured, all perfect, all blind.

Consider this...

- In this poem there is a constant juxtaposition of life and death, made real by the juxtaposition of contrasting realities, for example, the "fox" and the "quail." Identify as many contrasting realities as you can, culminating with the last one, in the final verse. What impact does the placement of these words have on the poem?

- What does the poet mean by "the wounded ghost of an old hunger"?

- What do you think about the combination of the words "messy" and "resurrection"? How does each word impact the other?

- At the end of the poem, how does the taxidermist feel about his own work? How does the poet want the reader to respond to the taxidermist's work? Do you think she succeeds in eliciting this emotion?

Bone

It was first dark when the plow turned it up.
Unsown, it came fleshless, mud-ruddled, nothing
but itself, the tendon's bored eye threading
a ponderous needle. And yet the pocked fist
of one end dared what was undone
in the strewing, defied the mouth of the hound
that dropped it.
            The whippoorwill began
again its dusk-borne mourning. I had never
seen what urgent wing disembodied
the voice, would fail to recognize its broken
shell or shadow or its feathers strewn
before me. As if afraid of forgetting,
it repeated itself, mindlessly certain.
                                        Here.
I threw the bone toward that incessant claiming,
and watched it turned by rote, end over end over end.

Consider this…

- "Poetry is what evaporates from all translations," wrote Robert Frost. This would also apply to paraphrasing a poem. Describe briefly, in prose, what happens in this poem. What would you say has "evaporated" from your description? In other words, what was poetic and no longer is?
- What does the poet discover through the experience of the poem? What does she do at the end with her discovery?
- Even though this poem is in free verse, with no obvious formal structure, are the words and phrases used the same way as the words and phrases you would use in casual conversation?
- What does the expression "literary phrasing" mean to you?

Spring Ice Storm

The forecast had not predicted it,
and its beginning, a calming, rumbled dusk

and pleasant lightning, she welcomed as harbinger
of rain. Than as night came she heard the world

relapse, slide backward into winter's insistent
tick and hiss. In the morning, she woke to a powerless

house, the baseboards cold, the sky blank,
mercury hardfallen as the ice and fixed

even at noon. The woodpile on the porch dwindled
to its last layer; she had not replenished it

for a month and could see beyond it windblown ice
in the shed where the axe angled Excalibur-like,

frozen in the wood. Still, she didn't worry
beyond the fate of the daffodils, green-sheathed,

the forsythia and quince already bloomed out—
knowing this couldn't last. But by afternoon

she did begin feeding the fire in the cast-iron
stove ordinary things she thought she could replace,

watching through the small window of isinglass
the fast-burning wooden spoons, picture frames,

then the phone book and stack of old almanacs—
forgotten predictions and phases of the moon—

before resorting to a brittle wicker rocker,
quick as dried grass to catch, bedframes and slats,

ladderback chairs, the labor of breaking them up
against the porch railing its own warming.

Feverlike, the freeze broke after two days,
and she woke to a melting steady as the rain

had been. The fire she had tended more carefully
than the household it had consumed she could now

let go out, and she was surprised at how little
she mourned the rooms heat-scoured, readied for spring.

Consider this…

- Both sound and imagery play powerful roles in this poem. Focus on each couplet and see how pairs of sounds reinforce each other, for example: "harbinger" and "heard," "insistent" and "hiss."
- Though not instances of strict alliteration or assonance, these resonances are important to any poem. Can you explain why? Find as many of them as you can.
- This poem—as all good poems—can be read on more than one level. What is the physical occurrence described by the poem?
- Might the poem be seen as a sustained metaphor for a different type of event? What event would that be?

Surface Hunting

You always washed artifacts
at the kitchen sink, your back
to the room, to me, to the mud

you'd tracked in from whatever
neighbor's field had just been plowed.
Spearpoints, birdpoints, awls, and leaf-

shaped blades surfaced from the turned earth
as though from beneath some thicker
water you tried to see into.

You never tired, you told me, of the tangible
past you could admire, turn over
and over in your hand—the first

to touch it since the dead one that had
worked the stone. You lined bookshelves
and end tables with them; obsidian,

quartz, flint, they measured the hours
you'd spent with your head down, searching
for others, and also the hours

of my own solitude—collected,
prized, saved alongside those
artifacts for so long lost.

Consider this...

- Do you think the use of tercets and staggered lines plays a significant role in the poem?
- How would you read the poem, if it had been written as prose, in a single paragraph?
- What kind of artifacts does the persona in the poem collect? At the end of the poem, these artifacts become metaphors. For what?
- What characteristics do these metaphors and the reality they bring to life share?

Drought

I began to understand
        its severity when glassy

crows came shameless, panting at last
        to the birdbath, and when the locusts

fell to the ground, another failed
        crop. The street lay empty all day,

and the river grew thinner, its spine
        showing through. Only butterflies

thrived—the still air cleft by their
        repeating patterns, the feathering

wings of swallowtails, monarchs;
        I learned from their bright emersion

to rely, for a while, only
        on the eye, the dry horizon.

Consider this...

- What effect does the use of the first person have at the onset of the poem? Why do you think the poet used "I" once more, close to the end of the poem, but nowhere else?

- There is a repeated consonant sound in the fourth and fifth couplet—thinner, through, thrived. What is the effect of this alliteration? What crucial word, not included but implied in the poem, starts with this same sound? Do you think that its meaning is being transmitted subconsciously to the reader?

- What effect does the assonance in the closing couplet—rely, eye, dry—have on the reader?

- Does the poem end in hope or in desolation? Is there an element of both? Support your answer by identifying those images in the poem that convey either or each of these sentiments.

Artifact

For three years you lived in your house
just as it was before she died: your wedding
portrait on the mantel, her clothes hanging
in the closet, her hair still in the brush.
You have told me you gave it all away
then, sold the house, keeping only the confirmation
cross she wore, her name in cursive chased
on the gold underside, your ring in the same

box, those photographs you still avoid,
and the quilt you spread on your borrowed bed—
small things. Months after we met, you told me she had
made it, after we had slept already beneath its loft
and thinning, raveled pattern, as though beneath
her shadow, moving with us, that dark, that soft.

Consider this…

- Is this poem primarily about (1) a person, (2) a thing, (3) a relationship, (4) an experience, or (5) an idea? Describe how the verses relate to each of these, and explain which of the four predominates.

- In what ways does this poem fulfill the characteristics of a sonnet? Why is the sonnet divided into two stanzas? What occurs between line 8 and line 9 to justify the separation?

- Do the words "dark" and "soft" reinforce each other? In other words, do they intensify their emotional impact on you, as the reader, or do they contrast each other, revealing two different aspects of an experience? Explain your answer.

Buying the Painted Turtle

Two boys, not quite men, pretended to let it go
only to catch it again and again. And the turtle,
equally determined, each time gave
its heart to escape them. We were near
the base of the old dam where the river
became a translucent, hissing wall, fixed
in falling, where, by the size of it, the turtle
had long trusted its defense, the streaming

algae, green, black, red—the garden of its spine—
not to fail it. They held it upside down,
the yellow plastron exposed; they hoisted it
over their heads like a trophy. I left it
to you to do the bargaining, exchange
the money for us to save it, let it go;

fast, it disappeared into deeper
water, returning to another present,
where the boulders cut the current to cast
safer shadows of motionlessness. We were
already forgotten, then, like most gods
after floods recede, after fevers break.

We did not talk about what we had bought—
an hour, an afternoon, a later death,
worth whatever we had to give for it.

Consider this…

- This poem is the closing poem in the collection *Late Wife*. Consider some other closing poems in other collections you've read. Do you see any common characteristics?

- What characteristics about life and death does this poem bring forth?

- Why is the turtle the main figure in the poem? Would the poem have worked just as well if the poet had selected another creature?

- Pick out those images in the poem that connote the idea of time and its passage, whether directly or indirectly.

- How is the idea of purchasing—buying, paying for—used to point toward a different, intangible value? What value is that?

At Home and Ranging Wide: The Poetry of Claudia Emerson

Claudia Emerson possesses the three essentials for making poems that matter: passion, precision, and the sense that her poems are absolutely necessary to her vision and her life. That imperative makes these poems necessary to readers as well, the great advantage of a grounded craft. Perhaps this also connects to Emerson's having come later to poetry than is usually the case; she served a considerable apprenticeship in what some call the real world, working at the kind of jobs (mail carrier, bookstore clerk) most people live by. Academia came later: the MFA from UNC Greensboro, residency teaching, adjunct teaching, even an unlikely but valued stint as dean of a girls' boarding school—then five prize-winning volumes of poems and an endowed professorship at Mary Washington University. All these experiences, along with the years growing up and living out a first marriage in the same small Virginia town among mythy tendrils of stories that cling to the oldest families and the land they knew, have shaped Emerson into a genuinely original poet who yet holds the English literary tradition close.

Like most early works, Emerson's first collection, *Pharaoh, Pharaoh,* is primarily a gathering of short lyrics. Even so, in poem after poem, a narrative thread catches us up. The poem "Auction," for example, surprises with detail that sketches the past lives and emotions of the farmer and his wife, whose possessions are being sold. Despite its brevity, the poem offers all the elements we need in order to grasp identity and experience. In "The Taxidermist," through the meditative voice of a man who remakes dead animals, we are exposed to the disturbing, matter-of-fact cast of his mind. "Timepiece," which also appears in this first book, melds narrative, extended metaphor, and lyric into a potent mix that prefigures what will come next for this poet.

Pinion: an Elegy is a masterful handling of story, song, lament, and celebration forged into an iron web of kinship, history, land, and longing. Here we find longer, richer lines, linked poems that narrate one story in many ways, dense with metaphor and interior music. Told alternately in the voices of a brother and sister aging on an isolated tobacco farm in the 1920s, the poems are rituals of passage and stasis. In them we recognize the almost mythic power that poetry can summon, and we remember that power long after the book is closed.

Emerson's third book, *Late Wife*, which earned her the Pulitzer Prize, turns in a completely different direction. It is the story of a divorce (after twenty years of marriage), of new love found and a new marriage made. Titled "Divorce Epistles," the first section relives, in tightly crafted lines—usually staggered three-line stanzas addressed to her ex-husband—the poet's old life. The poems recreate the world that left her, their raveling relationship, and a final, bitter grief that, nevertheless, keeps a difficult tenderness.

Two further sections follow: "Breaking Up the House," which focuses on women who are cut off and isolated, and the final section, titled "Late Wife, Letters to Kent," composed primarily of loose, often subtly slant-rhymed sonnets. Here, the poems address the poet's new husband, a widower whose first wife's death haunts the early days of the new marriage. The book's title assumes its full meaning in this section: the writer was lately the wife of another, she comes late to this marriage, and her husband's late wife is benignly present in many of the poems. We find this particularly evident in the poem

"Artifact," where the husband tells his new wife that the quilt on their bed was made by his first, late wife.

> ...after we had slept already beneath its loft
> and raveled, thinning pattern, as though beneath
> her shadow, moving with us, that dark, that soft.

There is sweetness in the new wife's exploration of what remains of her predecessor in the house they will leave, in the car, in the air. It is a making peace, a labor of understanding.

The volume ends with equal tenderness. In the closing poem "Buying the Painted Turtle," we find the poet and her husband walking on a riverbank, where they come upon two boys tormenting a turtle. The couple pays the tormentors for the turtle, in order to let it go back to its river. The poignant closing lines of the poem express the sum of the mature joy in their relationship.

> We did not talk about what we had bought—
> an hour, an afternoon, a later death,
> worth whatever we had to give for it.

Figure Studies, Emerson's fourth book, takes yet another direction. The extended first section, preceded by an introductory poem about a dress mannequin that has been discarded in a car repair "body" shop, is titled "All Girls School." Drawing on images from her own days as a student and her brief time as an administrator of just such a school, the poet creates a twenty-five-page series of lyric poems in two-line stanzas. Taken together, the poems confirm the truth of the section's epigraph, a quotation from Sir George Frazer's *The Golden Bough*. In referring to young women who are isolated from a group, shut away from influence so as to be made powerless, Frazer says, "In short, she is rendered harmless by being, in electrical language, insulated."

The girls school poems are about insulation and its costs. They are also about the inner world into which these protected girls might nevertheless withdraw. They discover such a world in the poem "Biology Lesson," where the reader sees that the students can draw more than one kind of knowledge from this schooling. While observing a plodding turtle,

> ...they are convinced of another
> sky into which it withdraws, not to become
>
> invisible, but to soar, fearless, inside
> itself—small dome of safe, starless heaven.

The other shorter poems in this collection deal with the lives of the women these girls will likely become, the women their mothers and grandmothers may have become. Taken as a whole, *Figure Studies* is a book about gender, about herded simmering young girls, and about women's lives frozen in more ways than one. From the discarded mannequin in the body shop to the preserved wax form of the Medical Venus in the Museo la Specola in Florence of the final poem, the book explores similarities and differences among figures of paralysis.

The poet Eleanor Wilner has described Emerson's work as "cool in appraisal, warm in affection." It is a perceptive assessment, applicable to the wide array of Emerson's books. Her mastery of range and subject—from the autobiographical to the magical, from narrative to lyric, from nuanced formal practice to musical free verse—sets Emerson additionally apart. Each book is different from the others, yet in all of them there is a steadiness of vision and tone, a persistent certainty.

It is important to note, too, this poet's ability to show each collection as more than a gathering of separate poems. Every volume creates what Robert Frost called the final poem of any book: the book itself as a coherent whole, a formal construct complete with its own arc and dramatic tension. It is an achievement enhanced by Emerson's wonderful ear for the muted music of the English language and her perfect grasp of metaphor's possibilities. Claudia Emerson shines as one of the nation's finest poets.

Betty Adcock

Kelly Cherry

2010-2012

KELLY CHERRY:
A Biographical Sketch

Kelly Cherry was born in Baton Rouge, Louisiana, to an intensely musical family. Her parents were violinists who specialized in string quartets. When she was nine the family moved to Chesterfield County, now part of Richmond, Virginia, where her father taught at Richmond Professional Institute (now Virginia Commonwealth University). He was also cofounder of the Richmond Symphony Orchestra.

After college, Kelly Cherry did graduate work in philosophy at the University of Virginia. She met her first husband, the sculptor Jonathan Silver, at the University of North Carolina-Greensboro, where she received her MFA, then moved with him to New York City, where they lived until the marriage ended in 1969. In 1977, Ms. Cherry moved to Wisconsin, where she taught at UW-Madison until 1999, when she retired as Eudora Welty Professor Emerita of English and Evjue-Bascom Professor Emerita in the Humanities.

A prolific writer, Kelly Cherry is the author of over twenty works of fiction, poetry, and nonfiction, as well the translator of two classical plays. Her most recently published titles are *The Woman Who,* a collection of short fiction (Boson Books, 2010), *The Retreats of Thought: Poems* (LSU Press, 2009), and *Girl in a Library: On Women Writers & the Writing Life* (BkMk Press, Univ. of MO-KC). Her short fiction has been reprinted in *Best American Short Stories, Prize Stories: The O. Henry Awards, The Pushcart Prize*, and *New Stories from the South*, and she has won three PEN/Syndicated Fiction Awards. In 2000, her collection *The Society of Friends:*

Stories (Univ. of Missouri Press, 1999) received the Dictionary of Literary Biography Award for the best volume of short stories published in 1999.

Kelly Cherry was the first recipient of the Hanes Poetry Prize given by the Fellowship of Southern Writers for a body of work. Other awards include fellowships from the National Endowment for the Arts and the Rockefeller Foundation, the Bradley Major Achievement (Lifetime) Award, a Distinguished Alumnus Award, three Wisconsin Arts Board fellowships, and selection as a Wisconsin Notable Author. In 2010, she was a Director's Visitor at the Institute for Advanced Study in Princeton.

Kelly Cherry was selected Virginia's Poet Laureate in 2010, a position she held through June 2012. She lives on a small farm in Virginia, with her husband, the fiction writer Burke Davis III. She is currently working on two collections of poetry and two of short fiction and looks forward to writing another novel.

Wishing I Could Bring You Back and See Things More Clearly This Time Around

(Jonathan Silver, sculptor, d. 1992)

I wish that I could bring you back, and you
would be as young as you were then, excited
about the world and art, and loving to
go on about both with me ready to write it
all down. I was enthralled by every word
you said, on any subject—though not always
agreeing and then you said I hadn't *heard*
you but I had, and I still do, some days,
when a painting speaks to me, or when the world
itself seems like a painting, or a sculpture
you might have made (a thing that can seem hurled
at the viewer, light and shade chiseled to pure
pain, as if pain were what we need to see
and what I failed to see, listening so intently).

Consider this…

- We often refer to the value of imagery in a poem. This particular poem, however, does not rely on images—at least not on the visual or even sensory kind. What poetic tools or tropes does the poem rely on? Why are they so effective?

- How many sentences make up the poem? What effect does the use of a single sentence for the last ten verses of the poem have on you, as the reader?

- Lyricism can be defined as the emotional thrust of a poem, made possible through its melodic qualities (cadence, linguistic harmonies, rhyme, rhythm). Where does the lyricism of this poem come from? How is it realized?

Waiting for the End of Time

Behind the window, in that room where rain
and wind were instrumentalists playing
on the windowpane, you were asleep, again,
and never heard the words that I was saying.
I didn't say them for you to hear, I said
them to your heart, that listening, third ear.

What anyone's heart knows is what has been bled
out of it...

It's February, a different year,
and spring seems something that a season might do
for the sheer delight of being sprung,
a kind of rhythm, a heartbeat, a *parlando*
(the words are spoken even though they're sung),
and everything is different now, except
time itself, which goes right on being kept.

Consider this…

- Look at the rhyme scheme of this poem and identify the form.
- What variations on that form has the poet incorporated? What, do you think, is the most effective deviation from it?
- Can you think of one or two words in English that have the same root as the Italian word in this poem: *parlando*? What meaning connects them?
- What does the inclusion of a word in a different language do for this poem?
- Foreign words surround us. Consider one that speaks to you, either because of its sound or its peculiar connotations, and write a poem (in English) that will allow you to use that word.

Woman Living Alone

A book on the bed,
radio turned to a classical station.

Raining or not raining, but if it is, the water rushes
into the bushes by the side of the brick house,

bridal wreath bushes, their white flowers
like snow in spring.

If it is not raining,
there may be a blue sky like a blessing

being pronounced over a meal, which,
though taken alone,

tastes of life.

Consider this…

- There are both an indoor and an outdoor scene in this poem. Visualize each scene by separating those verses that apply to one and those that apply to the other. Which images, sounds, or perceptions echo each other?

- How do these various perceptions reinforce the central emotion of the poem rather than distract from it?

- The poem uses alliteration in the second and third couplets, repeating the "b" sound in brick, bridal and bushes, and then it allows assonance to take over, with the "w" sounds found in white, flowers, and snow. Contrast these sounds; think of the way they impact the flow of the poem, the scene they recreate. Can you describe what they do?

- How does the poem achieve its unity? What do you think occurs in the last verse?

The Pines without Peer

The pines without peer
Are taller than air.

They grow in the sky,
Their roots in your eye.

And the tops of the pines wave
From the top of the sky, brave

As banners. And the tops
Of the pines are steps

To the high, wheeling
Stars. And your brain is reeling

And the trees are falling,
And you are falling

In a forest, pulled
Drawn, blinded, and mauled,

And you are the ground
And the wound

And the one wild sound.

Consider this…

- Read this poem aloud and pay special attention to its beat, enhanced by the use of couplets and by the rhyme scheme.

- How and where does the mood of the poem change?

- What is the effect of the repeated, somewhat flowing, present progressives (wheeling, reeling, falling, falling), followed by a succession of sturdier passive verbs (pulled, drawn, blinded, mauled)?

- Why is the "you" in the poem identified with "the ground…the wound…the one wild sound"?

My Mother's Father

lived in a sawmill, whittling
houses for strangers.
On Sunday he rowed to church
via bayou backwaters. All his daughters
dreamed of Ahab and Ulysses
(they were at that age).
They drifted like leaves pried from the riverbank.
Their bare limbs glowed in the late of day.
When twilight came, the woody cypress grew
shadows, and fairy rings
sprang up and disappeared
overnight.

Consider this…

- What is the common trait between Ahab and Ulysses, and why is it relevant to the poem? What words and phrases in the poem pull the reader toward that common experience?

- Is the sense of rootedness celebrated or bemoaned in the poem? In what ways?

- What does the word "whittling" bring to mind? In your view, why did the poet choose this word? What do you associate with its sound (not with its specific meaning)? Is sound crucial in the selection of a word for a poem? Does sound lead to meaning?

- What other words in the poem, do you think, were chosen mostly for their sound? Support your answer.

In the Field

The kind of day
when everything is so still
it seems to be an image of itself,
a mirrored photograph,
and only the secret lives of insects,
intense and determined among the leaves and grass,
enact the motivations of the real.

In this shadowless light
of uncontaminated noon, a fence post
gleams as if gilded, church spire where there
                                        is no church.
The impossibly beautiful blossoms of the crab apple
have spilled onto the ground,
an imperturbable pool of pink and white.
This illusion of the real, almost real.

Consider this…

- Notice the contrast that exists in this poem between sensory perceptions and abstractions of reality. Can you list at least three of each?

- Why do you think the poet has chosen to use these two sets of words? How do they bounce off each other and enhance the poem?

- What hour of day is it in the poem? Why do you think the poet has focused on this particular hour? What distinguishes it from the rest of the day?

- If you were to focus on a time of day, which one would it be? What mood does that hour of the day create in you? Is it still or dynamic? Write a poem that recreates this hour.

The Heat Down South (Richmond, 1955)

The heat does something wonderful
and difficult for Northerners to grasp.
It says a silent benediction,
it houses us in torpor.
A halo of humidity
surrounds the porch, the people
are robed in sweat and none contrive
to do much more than read a magazine.
To turn the fan to "on" is strenuous
and so is reaching for a beer. Night
may bring relief or trouble but
tonight's forever from now.
A six-foot floor-fan shuffles the air,
which doesn't cool the room,
and no one stirs, and nothing else
is moving. Telephones won't ring:
Forget the will to power,
we haven't the will to say hello.
No one knocks. You are secured
from all assaults upon your consciousness
and there is nothing to keep you from
imagining a wiser nation might
arise among the fields and woods,
the birds at liberty,
the lions lying down with lambs.

Consider this...

- This poem presents a litany of minor events that characterize a hot summer day—yet the list is not prosaic, it does not sound or feel like prose. Why is that?

- Take several examples from the poem—of things that are occurring—and rewrite them as prose. Where does the difference lie? What did the poet do with the words—their order, their juxtaposition, their selection, perhaps, based on sound—to turn the information into a poem?

- Think of the difference between to *denote* and to *connote*. Discuss how this difference parallels the distinction between prose and poetry.

- Focus on the last seven verses of the poem. What do the following words and phrases—"assault," "imagining," "arise," "fields and woods," "birds at liberty," and "lions lying down with lambs"—denote? What do they connote?

A Farm in Virginia near the North Carolina Boundary

The shadow of a grassblade falls upon the worm.
The blue-tailed skink slips in under the door.
This life as lived on a southern farm
with fruit trees (apple orchard; fig and pear).
Scarlet tanagers let themselves be seen
from time to time. Rabbits and deer devour
the season's garden. Bees linger at the screen.
Some days the sky is low and seems to lower,
and others blue, with clouds a rickrack trim,
or black with blowing rain that stills and hushes
the birds while large-mouth bass and turtles swim
in the muddy-bottomed pond; rain rattles bushes.
It's busy here; a lot is going on
most all the time and now and then scarlet
tanagers, bright baubles in the morning sun,
and shy despite the gaudy garb of harlot,
fly by, a pair; house wrens flock at the feeder.
The bees that fumble at the sill will swarm.
A cardinal relaxes in a cedar.
This is life on a small southeastern farm.
A blue tailed skink slips out under the door.
The shadow of a grassblade crosses the worm.

Consider this...

- Compare the mood of this poem with the mood of "The Heat Down South." How are they different?

- How does the poet achieve a sense of motion in this poem? Is it a hectic or a tranquil motion?

- Select the more active images of the poem and set them alongside the more passive ones. How does the poet distribute these images? How does their placement make you feel? In other words, just when you are about to get carried away by the activities on the farm, what does the poet do to encourage the opposite sensation?

- What is the reason for the reappearance of certain characters in the poem (the bee, the tanager, the skink, the worm)?

- What effect does the repetition of the opening verses at the end of the poem have?

"That Complicated Country": Kelly Cherry's Love Poetry

I won't tell you the name of the school. The students were middle and high schoolers and I had been invited to speak and recite and meet a few classes. I performed these duties to the best of my fragile abilities and a week after I departed I received a review of my appearance in the student newspaper. It began, "Fred Chappell, a short man with gray hair…"

Ouch. How this cold-water description dashed my spirits! The young lady who wrote it was woefully accurate; I am a short man with gray hair. But I had hoped that I would make a more spirited impression.

Then I thought, "But how disappointed she must have been! Expecting a personage of *poetic dimension*, she had to settle for a small, rather pedantic fellow, so much less than the figure she had imagined in reading my love poems."

Kelly Cherry is a love poet. She is also a philosophical, narrative, satirical, and elegiac poet, but romantic love is one of her abiding themes, as in the poem called "A Song."

> How he loved me! trembled
>
> if I touched his hand.
>
> I saw his quick eyes glittering
>
> in the night.
>
> I saw him strip off his skin.
>
> And white bones clattering
>
> he fled into the night.

This brief lyric begins tenderly but quickly turns ominous, "quick eyes glittering," and it ends mysteriously and scarily. Has the lover revealed a demonic side of himself? Has he transformed into Death personified?

That's the way to write an electrifying love poem. And if Ms. Cherry had visited the same school I did, she would not have disappointed. Slender, graceful, witty, attractive, she would have captivated my young friends there as she had already captivated so many others with her glamour, intelligence, and bewitching personality. She was, is, and always shall be intriguing—as intriguing as the poem titled "A Song."

Here is another love poem. It belongs to an ancient tradition of love poems called a "complaint," in which the poet cries out against the cruelty of fate. In the case of this particular love complaint, the speaker may be found to be the victim of her own passion:

> I will cut out my heart
> It has tricked me into desire
> Betrayed its body and myself
> Been a liar
>
> I will cut out my heart
>
> It has urged me to hope
> Leapt like a spring and stolen
> The end of my rope
>
> For this one last time
> I will cut out my heart
> It has bound me to love
> And pulled me apart

This poem, "I Will Cut Out My Heart," reads as if it might have been written in Elizabethan times by Thomas Carew or Christopher Marlowe. Yet it imitates no school or manner of writing; it is no exercise of the kind that poets undertake to keep their skills sharp in the way that pianists practice scales and basketball players run passing drills. It is heartfelt passion, a poem that cried out to be set down in the cleanest possible terms. Yet it is elegant, pure in tone and simple in form, and for all the pain it expresses, it stands a beautiful object in itself. The feeling it expresses is common to ten thousand Nashville country music songs; but its use of words is too powerful for such sentimental presentation. It is a lyric, not a tune.

Here is another, called "She Remembers the Tears":

> She remembers the tears
> the sun drew from her
> on a hot day, the way
> panic strikes and sears
> the soul, a small puff
> of smoke, but enough
>
> so it disappears:
> a smudge of ash
> on a round stone, and none
> where she used to weep tears.
> The burned-out ravine
> is serene.

Time has passed since the situation of "I Will Cut Out My Heart." The pains and furies of unsuccessful love have been survived and now the speaker recalls a dreadful period in the past. But has the person really survived? It seems the soul has been blasted by fear and sorrow until nothing is left but "a smudge of ash / on a round stone." The experience of this love has been like a stroke of lightning and the poet may be suggesting that we recall the ancient Greek myth of Semele. Semele was a woman who had been seduced by Zeus, the greatest of the gods, in a human form. When she prayed that she might see him as himself in all of his splendor she was consumed as by lightning. In Ms. Cherry's poem the result is so powerful that it not only destroys the soul, it even explodes the surrounding landscape into a "burned-out ravine."

Perhaps it is unwise to desire to know the full force of love—yet is it not human nature to want to do so, even though the outcome may be grievous?

We would not come to love if it did not promise pleasure and other rewards besides. A famous Spanish thinker observed that when we are in love, our faculties are made keener; we see things more closely, we hear and taste more vividly. It is a condition that affects all the senses and brings the world nearer to us, as in "Love":

> In the attention it pays to each detail,
> In its frailty and flexibility,
> In the way it seeks out a new trail
> While stumbling repeatedly upon the old,
>
> You will know love, and know
> That what it cannot fail to do
> Is render even this late scene
> In all its abundance,
>
> The red-tailed hawk overhead,
> Spongy moss springing from wet bark,
> The sound of your own walking
> Through these autumnal woods.

"Love" exhibits the achievement that quiet presentation can afford. There are three stanzas but only one sentence. The voice is muted as it begins describing in abstract language certain qualities of the state of being in love. Then the image of a trail is introduced, though it is not placed in a specific location. In the last stanza we discover that the trail is to be found "in these autumnal woods" in which aspects of nature are brought sharply into focus by the regenerated senses. One figure from nature is the speaker herself; she is aware of her presence here and we understand that she is older now, a part of the autumn, and is enjoying the contentment that a fresh understanding of the world has brought about.

I cannot see that the poem is anything less than perfect. It fulfills its modest intentions to the limits. In ancient times it might have been sung by a chorus of women in a tragic drama.

Ms. Cherry is a poet of many different moods and subjects. Her formal training in philosophical analysis opens the doors to topics in history, science, religion, mythology, music, and classical and modern literatures. She is also skillful in the use of autobiographical materials and, as she has traveled widely and lived profoundly, these furnish her with a nearly endless supply of matter to write about.

Such subjects are complex and demand the thoughtful treatment she gives them. It is mostly for reasons of space that I have written here about her love poetry. Yet, after all, love is as complex and fruitful a subject as any historical incident or mathematical theory. In one of her longer poems she refers to love as "that complicated country." She has put much of her tireless industry and brilliant insight into discovering and revealing large tracts of love's unmapped territories.

In "Reading, Dreaming, Hiding" Ms. Cherry gives us a scene of two lovers in a room. The weather outside is stormy and makes the shelter of the room and its silence even cozier. The lovers are together yet separate from each other. They are engaged in different activities, yet both are doing the same thing. They are silent but communicating with warm, contained ardency, yet without speaking. Poetry is fulfilled through the tension experienced by the lovers in the poem—and by us, with them—a tension between what is latent, immediate, transitory, and what endures, yet remains hidden from the eye.

You were reading. I was dreaming
The color blue. The wind was hiding
In the trees and rain was streaming
Down the window, full of darkness.

Rain was dreaming in the trees. You
Were full of darkness. The wind was streaming
Down the window, the color blue.
I was reading and hiding.

The wind was full of darkness and rain
Was streaming in the trees and down the window.
The color blue was full of darkness, dreaming
In the wind and trees. I was reading you.

As in her other works, Ms. Cherry's fine economy informs not only her technique and presentation, but her perception. Many things are happening in the poem, though they happen with preternatural quietness. If a painter undertook to represent the theme, she would emphasize the sense of stillness and try for an effect that certain painters like Millet and Rembrandt are able to achieve—to portray a single moment that is eternal.

Fred Chappell

About the Authors and the Editor

Betty Adcock is the author of six poetry collections, most recently, *Slantwise* (LSU Press). Among her numerous awards are the Poets' Prize, the Hanes Award from the Fellowship of Southern Writers, and fellowships from the Guggenheim Foundation and the National Endowment for the Arts. She was Kenan Writer-in-Residence at Meredith College and has held professorships in other universities. She is a faculty member of the Warren Wilson College MFA Program and lives in North Carolina.

Fred Chappell, former Poet Laureate of North Carolina, is the author of twelve books of poetry, two story collections, and eight novels. His work *Dagon* was named Best Foreign Book of the Year by the Académie Française. Other literary awards include the Bollingen Prize, the Aiken Taylor Award, and the T. S. Eliot Prize. His most recent poetry collection is *Shadow Box* (LSU Press).

Cathryn Hankla is the author of eleven books of poetry and fiction including *Last Exposures: a sequence of poems* (LSU Press) and *Fortune Teller Miracle Fish: stories* (Michigan State University Press). Various awards for her work include a Virginia Commission for the Arts fellowship, a PEN Syndicated Fiction Award, the James Boatright III Prize in Poetry, and a first place award for her new collection of stories from the New York Book Festival. She directs the Jackson Center for Creative Writing at Hollins University and serves as poetry editor for *The Hollins Critic*.

Edward Lull is a Life Member of The Poetry Society of Virginia, having served four terms as its president. He has published three books of poetry: *Cabin Boy to Captain: a Sea Story*; *Where Giants Walked*, and *The Sailors: Birth of a Navy*. His most recent book is *Bits and Pieces: A Memoir,* published in 2011. He co-edited, with Carolyn Kreiter-Foronda, the first *Four Virginia Poets Laureate: A Teaching Guide*, published in 2006. Lull was the 2012 recipient of the Emyl Jenkins Award from the James River Writers Organization "for inspiring a love of writing and writing education in Virginia."

Kevin Everod Quashie teaches cultural studies in the department of Afro-American Studies at Smith College. He has published three books: *New Bones*, an anthology of contemporary African American literature, *(Un)Becoming the Subject*, a study of black women and cultural theory, and most recently, *The Sovereignty of Quiet* (Rutgers University Press), which considers the concept of quiet in the context of how we think about black culture.

Sofia M. Starnes, Virginia's current poet laureate, is the author of five poetry collections, most recently *Fully Into Ashes* (Wings Press) and *Love and the Afterlife* (Franciscan University Press). She is the recipient of a Fellowship from the Virginia Commission for the Arts and numerous poetry commendations, including the Transcontinental Poetry Editor's Prize, the Rainer Maria Rilke Poetry Prize, the Marlboro Review Editor's Poetry Award, and the Virginia Writers Club Outstanding Achievement

Award in Poetry. Sofia serves as Poetry Editor and Poetry Book Review Editor of the *Anglican Theological Review* and mentors writers through her professional service, Creative Writing Critiques.

Dr. Charles W. Steger, the 15th president of Virginia Tech, has greatly expanded Virginia Tech's research and outreach programs beyond the main Blacksburg campus. His support of the arts is patent in numerous ways, most recently in the creation of the new Center for the Arts at Virginia Tech. On a personal level, Dr. Steger sponsors the Steger Prize for Poetry, the largest poetry award given to an undergraduate in the United States.

Acknowledgments

Rita Dove:

"The Event" from *Thomas and Beulah: Poems*, Carnegie Mellon University Press, Pittsburgh, PA © 1986 by Rita Dove. Reprinted by permission of the author.
"Persephone Abducted," "Exit," and "Golden Oldie" from *Mother Love*, W.W. Norton & Company, New York, NY © 1995 by Rita Dove. Reprinted by permission of the author.
"Lady Freedom Among Us" from *On the Bus with Rosa Parks*, W.W. Norton & Company, New York, NY © 1999 by Rita Dove. Reprinted by permission of the author.
"Against Flight" and "I have been a stranger in a strange land" from *American Smooth*, W. W. Norton & Company, New York, NY © 2004 by Rita Dove. Reprinted by permission of the author.
"Ach, Wien" from *Sonata Mulattica*, W. W. Norton & Company, New York, NY © 2009 by Rita Dove. Reprinted by permission of the author.

Carolyn Kreiter-Foronda:

"A Basket of Potatoes" and "Contrary Visions in the Gallery, White on White" from *Contrary Visions*, Scripta Humanistica, Potomac, MD ©1998 by Carolyn Kreiter-Foronda. Reprinted by permission of the author.
"By the Bay" from *Death Comes Riding*, SCOP Publications, Catonsville, MD © 1999 by Carolyn Kreiter-Foronda. Reprinted by permission of the author.

"You Don't Need Binoculars to Be a Bird Watcher" and "Hurricane" from *River Country*, San Francisco Bay Press, San Francisco, CA © 2008 by Carolyn Kreiter-Foronda. Reprinted by permission of the author.
"Solitude" appeared in the *Comstock Review*, "Calla Lillies" and "The Two Fridas, 1939" appeared in *Nimrod International Journal* © by Carolyn Kreiter-Foronda. "Calla Lillies" also was anthologized in *An Endless Skyway: Poetry from the State Poets Laureate of America,* Ice Cube Books, 2011. Reprinted by permission of the author.

Claudia Emerson:

"Auction" and "The Taxidermist" from *Pharaoh, Pharaoh*, LSU Press, Baton Rouge, LA © 1997 by Claudia Emerson. Reprinted by permission of LSU Press.
"Bone" from *Pinion, an Elegy,* LSU Press, Baton Rouge, LA © 2002 by Claudia Emerson. Reprinted by permission of LSU Press.
"Spring Ice Storm" from *Figure Studies,* LSU Press, Baton Rouge, LA © 2008 by Claudia Emerson. Reprinted by permission of LSU Press.
"Surface Hunting," "Drought," "Artifact," and "Buying the Painted Turtle" from *Late Wife,* LSU Press, Baton Rouge, LA © 2005 by Claudia Emerson. Reprinted by permission of LSU Press.

Kelly Cherry:

"Wishing I Could Bring You Back and See Things More Clearly This Time Around" from *Rising Venus*, LSU Press, Baton Rouge, LA © 2002 by Kelly Cherry.

Reprinted by permission of LSU Press.
"Waiting for the End of Time" and "Woman Living Alone" from *God's Loud Hand,* LSU Press, Baton Rouge, LA ©1993 by Kelly Cherry. Reprinted by permission of LSU Press.
"The Pines without Peer" and "My Mother's Father" from *Relativity: A Point of View,* Carnegie Mellon University Press, Pittsburgh, PA © 2000 by Kelly Cherry. Reprinted by permission of the author.
"In the Field," "The Heat Down South (Richmond, 1955)," and "A Farm in Virginia near the North Carolina Boundary" from *Hazard and Prospect,* LSU Press, Baton Rouge, LA © 2007 by Kelly Cherry. Reprinted by permission of LSU Press.

Photo credits:

Rita Dove: Photo by Fred Viebahn
Carolyn Kreiter-Foronda: Photo by Dick Welton
Claudia Emerson: Photo by Kent Ippolito
Kelly Cherry: Photo by Burke Davis III